Conference on Empirical Methods in Natural Language Processing (EMNLP 2025)

AA004803

Tutorial Abstracts

Suzhou, China
8 November 2025

ISBN: 979-8-3313-2868-9

Printed from e-media with permission by:

Curran Associates, Inc.
57 Morehouse Lane
Red Hook, NY 12571

Some format issues inherent in the e-media version may also appear in this print version.

Copyright© (2025) by the Association for Computational Linguistics
All rights reserved.

Printed with permission by Curran Associates, Inc. (2026)

For permission requests, please contact the Association for Computational Linguistics
at the address below.

Association for Computational Linguistics
209 N. Eighth Street
Stroudsburg, Pennsylvania 18360

Phone: 1-570-476-8006
Fax: 1-570-476-0860

acl@aclweb.org

Additional copies of this publication are available from:

Curran Associates, Inc.
57 Morehouse Lane
Red Hook, NY 12571 USA
Phone: 845-758-0400
Fax: 845-758-2633
Email: curran@proceedings.com
Web: www.proceedings.com

EMNLP 2025

The 2025 Conference on Empirical Methods in Natural Language Processing

Tutorial Abstracts

November 8, 2025

©2025 Association for Computational Linguistics

Introduction

Welcome to the Tutorial Session of EMNLP 2025!

Building on the rapid progress in NLP, this year's tutorials at EMNLP 2025 will provide the audience with comprehensive overviews of seven cutting-edge topics by experts in these areas: efficient inference for large language models, instruction tuning, spoken conversational agents, code intelligence in language models, multilingual LLM expansion, neuro-symbolic approaches, and continual learning.

As in recent years, the process of soliciting, reviewing, and selecting tutorials was a collaborative effort across ACL, EACL, NAACL, and EMNLP. Each tutorial proposal underwent an evaluation by a panel of three reviewers, who assessed them based on multiple criteria including clarity, preparedness, novelty, timeliness, instructor expertise, potential audience reach, open access to teaching materials, and diversity. Following this review process, seven tutorials were selected for EMNLP 2025. We also ensured that at least one of the instructors will be presenting in person at the conference, as it is a better experience for the attendees.

We would like to thank the tutorial authors for their contributions, the tutorial chairs across conferences for this coordinated effort, as well as the EMNLP conference organizers, especially the general chair Dirk Hovy.

EMNLP 2025 Tutorial Co-chairs
Valentina Pyatkin
Andreas Vlachos

Organizing Committee

General Chair

Dirk Hovy, Bocconi University

Tutorial Chairs

Valentina Pyatkin, Allen Institute for AI; University of Washington
Andreas Vlachos, University of Cambridge

Table of Contents

Efficient Inference for Large Language Models – Algorithm, Model, and System

Xuefei Ning, Guohao Dai, Haoli Bai, Lu Hou, Yu Wang and Qun Liu

The inference of LLMs incurs high computational costs, memory access overhead, and memory usage, leading to inefficiencies in terms of latency, throughput, power consumption, and storage.

To this end, this tutorial focuses on the increasingly important topic of ***Efficient Inference for LLMs*** and aims to *provide a systematic understanding of key facts and methodologies from a designer's perspective.* We start by introducing the basic concepts of modern LLMs, software and hardware. Following this, we define the efficiency optimization problem. To equip the audience with a designer's mindset, we briefly explain how to diagnose efficiency bottlenecks for a given workload on specific hardware.

After introducing the basics, we will introduce our full-stack taxonomy of efficient inference methods for LLMs. We will walk through each category of methodology, using one to three representative methods as examples for each leaf subcategory, elaborating on the design logic behind each method and which inefficiency factors they primarily address. Finally, we will wrap up with a takeaway summary, and future research directions.

Xuefei Ning, Research-Track Assistant Professor, Tsinghua University
email: `foxdoraame@gmail.com`
website: `https://nics-effalg.com/ningxuefei/`
Xuefei Ning is a research-track assistant professor with the Department of Electronic Engineering at Tsinghua University. She obtained her Ph.D. at Tsinghua University in 2021. Her research focuses on efficient deep learning. She has published 30+ papers in leading AI conferences and journals. She has published a Chinese book on efficient deep learning. She serves as a senior area chair for ACL 2025, an area chair for CVPR 2025 and ICLR 2026.

Guohao Dai, Associate Professor, Shanghai Jiao Tong University
email: `daiguohao@sjtu.edu.cn`
website: `https://dai.sjtu.edu.cn/pepledetail.html?id=218`
Guohao Dai is an associate professor with the Department of Electronic Information and Electrical Engineering at Shanghai Jiao Tong University.

Proceedings of the 2025 Conference on Empirical Methods in Natural Language Processing: Tutorial Abstracts, pages 1–3
November 8, 2025 ©2025 Association for Computational Linguistics

His research focuses on sparse computing, heterogeneous hardware computing, emerging hardware architecture, etc. He served as Co-Chair for the Ph.D. Forum at DAC 2024, TPC member for DAC 2024/DAC 2023/VLSID 2024. He received the Best Paper Award in ASP-DAC 2019, and Best Paper Nominations in DATE 2024/DATE 2023/DAC 2022/DATE 2018. He is the winner of the NeurIPS Billion-Scale Approximate Nearest Neighbor Search Challenge in 2021, and the recipient of the Outstanding PhD Dissertation Award of Tsinghua University in 2019.

Haoli Bai, Researcher, Huawei Technologies Co. Ltd.
email: `baihaoli@huawei.com`
website: `https://haolibai.github.io/`
Haoli Bai is a researcher at Huawei Noah's Ark Lab. He obtained his Ph.D. at the Chinese University of Hong Kong in 2021. His research focus is efficient deep learning with the purpose to minimize memory and computational requirements, particularly for large language models. He has published multiple research works on network quantization, pruning, and relevant topics, with applications on Huawei Ascend Chips and products. He obtained the ACML Best Student Paper Runner-up Award (2016), and has served as the PC member for top AI conferences (e.g., NeurIPS, ICML, ICLR).

Lu Hou, Researcher, Huawei Technologies Co. Ltd.
email: `houlu3@huawei.com`
website: `https://houlu369.github.io/`
Lu Hou is a researcher at Huawei Noah's Ark Lab. She obtained her Ph.D. from Hong Kong University of Science and Technology in 2019. Her research focuses on developing efficient deep learning models with lower memory and computation costs, especially for large pre-trained language and multimodal models. Her researches have been published at leading conferences (e.g., NeurIPS, ICML, ICLR, ACL, EMNLP) as well as been applied to various chips, products and LLMs at Huawei.

Yu Wang, Full Professor, Tsinghua University
email: `yu-wang@tsinghua.edu.cn`
website: `https://nicsefc.ee.tsinghua.edu.cn/people/YuWang`
Yu Wang is a professor, an IEEE fellow, the chair of the Department of Electronic Engineering in Tsinghua University, the dean of the Institute for Electronics and Information Technology in Tianjin, and the vice dean of the School of Information Science and Technology in Tsinghua University. His research interests include the application specific heterogeneous computing,

processing-in-memory, intelligent multi-agent system, and power/reliability aware system design methodology. He has published more than 90 journals (64 IEEE/ACM journals) and 270 conference papers in the areas of EDA, FPGA, VLSI Design, and Embedded Systems, with the Google Scholar citation over 22,000. He has received four best paper awards and 12 best paper nominations. He has been an active volunteer in the design automation, VLSI, and FPGA conferences. He is the co-founder of Deephi Tech (a leading deep learning solution provider), which is acquired by Xilinx (AMD) in 2018. He is also the promoter of Infinigence AI Tech (a leading AI infrastructure solution provider), which achieves industry-leading large language model inference performance on more than 10+ different chips.

Qun Liu, Huawei Technologies Co. Ltd.
email: `qun.liu@huawei.com`
website: `https://liuquncn.github.io/`
Qun Liu is the chief scientist of Speech and Language Computing of Huawei Noah's Ark Lab. He is formerly a professor of Dublin City University, the Theme Learder of NLP at the ADAPT Centre, Ireland, a professor & researcher & the leader of NLP research group in the Institute of Computing Technology , Chinese Academy of Sciences (ICT-CAS). He obtained his B.Sc., M.Sc. and Ph.D. degrees in the University of Science and Technology of China, ICT-CAS, and Peking University respectively. His research interests cover natural language processing, language modeling, machine translation, question answering, dialog, etc. His academic achievements include ICTCLAS Chinese word segmentation and POS tagging system, syntax-based statistical machine translation, neural machine translation, machine translation evaluation, etc. He has been the leader or a participant in several large-scale projects funded by Chinese government, Irish government or European Union. He has published 300+ papers in academic conferences or journals, with 20,000+ citations. He has supervised 50+ Master or Ph.D. students into completion. He has obtained Google Research Award (2012), first prize of Qian Weichang Award for Chinese Information Processing Science and Technology (2010), and second prize of China National Award for Science and Technology Progress (2015), ACL Best Long Paper Awards (2019), and ACL Outstanding Paper Awards (2022, 2024).

Advancing Language Models through Instruction Tuning: Recent Progress and Challenges

Zhihan Zhang, Renze Lou, Fangkai Jiao, Wenpeng Yin
and Meng Jiang

The capability of following instructions is a key dimension for AI systems. Therefore, in NLP, instruction tuning – the process of training language models to follow natural language instructions – has become a fundamental component of the model development pipeline. This tutorial addresses three critical questions within the field: (1) What are the current focal points in instruction tuning research? (2) What are the best practices in training an instruction-following model? (3) What new challenges have emerged? To answer these questions, the tutorial presents a systematic overview of recent advances in instruction tuning. It covers different stages in model training: supervised fine-tuning, preference optimization, and reinforcement learning. It introduces scalable strategies for building high-quality instruction data, explores approaches for training autonomous AI agents that handle complex real-world tasks, and discusses common criteria for evaluating instruction-following models. The audience will gain a comprehensive understanding of cutting-edge trends in instruction tuning and insights into promising directions for future research.

Zhihan Zhang, Applied Scientist, Amazon
email: `zzhihan@amazon.com`
website: `https://ytyz1307zzh.github.io`
Zhihan Zhang is an Applied Scientist at Amazon. He works on building intelligent AI agents powered by large language models for shopping applications. Zhihan earned his Ph.D. in Computer Science and Engineering from the University of Notre Dame, where his research centered around training instruction-following language models. Prior to that, Zhihan received his B.S. from Peking University. Zhihan has published over 30 papers in top NLP/ML conferences and journals, including ACL, EMNLP, ICLR, and NAACL.

Renze Lou, Ph.D. student, Department of Computer Science and Engineering, Pennsylvania State University

Proceedings of the 2025 Conference on Empirical Methods in Natural Language Processing: Tutorial Abstracts, pages 4–6
November 8, 2025 ©2025 Association for Computational Linguistics

email: renze.lou@psu.edu
website: https://renzelou.github.io
Renze Lou is a third-year Ph.D. student at Pennsylvania State University. His research focuses on empowering AI agents to assist in various professional domains. He has extensive research experience in instruction tuning and following, agentic systems, and AI4Research. Renze has (co-)authored papers at top-tier conferences, including ICLR, ICML, AAAI, ACL, and EMNLP. He has also completed research internships at Salesforce Research and Microsoft Research.

Fangkai Jiao, Ph.D. student, College of Computing and Data Science, Nanyang Technological University
email: fangkai002@e.ntu.edu.sg
website: https://jiaofangkai.com
Fangkai Jiao is a fourth-year PhD student at Nanyang Technological University and the Institute of Infocomm Research, A*STAR, Singapore. Prior to his PhD, he received his M.Eng. and B.Eng. from Shandong University. Fangkai's research focuses on weak-supervised training and data synthesis for machine reasoning and large language models. He has published several papers in top-tier conferences and journals, including ACL, EMNLP, ICLR, and TPAMI. He has also held research internships at DAMO Academy, Alibaba Group, Microsoft Research Asia, and Bytedance Seed Team.

Wenpeng Yin, Assistant Professor, Department of Computer Science and Engineering, Penn State University
email: wenpeng@psu.edu
website: https://www.wenpengyin.org
Wenpeng Yin is an Assistant Professor in the Department of Computer Science and Engineering at Penn State University, USA. Dr. Yin is working on AI to automate NLP research. He has experience presenting tutorials at ACL 2023, EMNLP 2023, KONVENS 2023, and EMNLP 2024. He led the workshop "WISE-Supervision" co-located with AKBC 2022 and the 1st and 2nd AI4Resarch Workshops at IJCAI 2024/AAAI 2025.

Meng Jiang, Associate Professor and Frank M. Freimann Collegiate Professor of Computer Science and Engineering, University of Notre Dame
email: mjiang2@nd.edu
website: http://www.meng-jiang.com
Meng Jiang is an Associate Professor and Frank M. Freimann Collegiate Professor of Computer Science and Engineering at the University of Notre

Dame. He is appointed as the Director of Foundation Models at the Lucy Family Institute for Data and Society as well as the Program Chair of ND-IBM Tech Ethics Lab. He is an Amazon Scholar. His research interests are data mining, machine learning, and natural language processing (NLP) for applications such as material discovery, recommender system, question answering, education, and mental health. His recent projects focus on knowledge-augmented NLP, instructed large language model (LLM), self-correct LLM, personalized LLM, unlearned LLM, graph data augmentation, and graph diffusion model. He has delivered 15 conference tutorials and organized ten workshops on these topics. He has received multiple best paper awards and awarded NSF CAREER.

Spoken Conversational Agents with Large Language Models

Huck Yang, Andreas Stolcke, and Larry P. Heck

Website: https://huckiyang.github.io/emnlp-25-tutorial

Spoken conversational agents are converging toward voice-native LLMs. This tutorial distills the path from cascaded ASR/NLU to end-to-end, retrieval- and vision-grounded systems. We frame adaptation of text LLMs to audio, cross-modal alignment, and joint speech–text training; review datasets, metrics, and robustness across accents; and compare design choices (cascaded vs. E2E, post-ASR correction, streaming). We link industrial assistants to current open-domain and task-oriented agents, highlight reproducible baselines, and outline open problems in privacy, safety, and evaluation. Attendees leave with practical recipes and a clear systems-level roadmap.

Huck Yang, Sr. Research Scientist, NVIDIA Research
email: `huckiyang@nvidia.com`
website: `https://huckiyang.github.io/`
Huck obtained his Ph.D. and M.Sc. from Georgia Institute of Technology, Atlanta, GA, supported by Wallace H. Coulter Fellowship and B.Sc, from National Taiwan University. Prior to joining NVIDIA, he was a scientist at Amazon and a research intern at Google and Hitachi. His primary research lies in the area of speech-language modeling, robust speech recognition, and multi-modal post-training alignments. He served as area chairs and committee members in IEEE ICASSP 2022 to 2025, EMNLP 2024, SLT 2024, and NAACL 2025. He has served in the IEEE SPS technical committee at Applied Signals Processing Systems (ASPS) and Data Collection Committee (DCC) since 2022. He received the best industry paper honoronable mentioned ACL 25 and best student paper nominee in Interspeech 23.

Andreas Stolcke, Distinguished AI Scientist/VP, Uniphore
email: `stolcke@icsi.berkeley.edu`
website: `https://www.linkedin.com/in/andreas-stolcke`
Andreas obtained his PhD from UC Berkeley, followed by senior researcher/scientist positions at SRI International, Microsoft, and Amazon, as well as an external

Proceedings of the 2025 Conference on Empirical Methods in Natural Language Processing: Tutorial Abstracts, pages 7–8
November 8, 2025 ©2025 Association for Computational Linguistics

fellow of the Berkeley International Computer Science Institute. He is currently a Distinguished AI Scientist/VP at Uniphore, where he is leading research on conversational AI. His interests include computational linguistics, language modeling, speech recognition, speaker recognition and diarization, and paralinguistics, with over 300 papers and patents in these areas. His open-source SRI Language Modeling Toolkit was widely used in academia. Andreas is a Fellow of the IEEE, the International Speech Communication Association, and the Asia-Pacific Artificial Intelligence Association, as well as an IEEE Distinguished Industry Speaker.

Larry Heck, Rhesa Screven Farmer Jr., Advanced Computing Concepts Chair, Georgia Institute of Technology,
email: larryheck@gatech.edu
website: https://larryheck.github.io/
Larry Heck is a Professor with joint appointments in ECE and Interactive Computing at the Georgia Institute of Technology, where he holds the Rhesa S. Farmer Advanced Computing Concepts Chair and is a Georgia Research Alliance Eminent Scholar. He is an IEEE Fellow and National Academy of Inventors Fellow, author of numerous papers, and holder of more than 50 U.S. patents. He previously served as CEO of Viv Labs and SVP at Samsung (2017–2021), leading Bixby in North America. From 2014–2017, he was Principal Scientist at Google, leading dialogue research. At Microsoft (2009–2014), he was Chief Scientist of Speech products, Distinguished Engineer in MSR, and co-founder of Cortana. Earlier, he was VP at Yahoo, VP of R&D at Nuance, and began his career at SRI, where his team pioneered deep learning in speech processing. He earned his PhD and MS in Electrical Engineering from Georgia Tech, and his BSEE from Texas Tech University.

NLP+Code: Code Intelligence in Language Models

Terry Yue Zhuo, Qian Liu, Zijian Wang
Wasi Uddin Ahmad, Binyuan Hui, Loubna Ben Allal

https://code-lm.github.io

Language models (LMs) like GPT and Claude have shown impressive abilities in a range of natural language processing (NLP) tasks. Among these tasks, code understanding and generation have quickly become one of the most popular applications of LMs, given its nature of executable logic forms. However, there is a practical understanding of how programming knowledge can be combined with natural language to automate software development. Moreover, recent studies also empirically demonstrate that code can be a better form for complex reasoning and agentic task automation, but they do not indicate their significance. In this tutorial, we deem such superior capabilities brought by code modeling as *Code Intelligence*, and aim to provide a coherent overview of recent advances in this topic. We will start by first providing preliminaries of training foundation models on code and their common practices. We will then focus on downstream tasks in the domain of code and their evaluations. Then, we will cover how code can contribute to advancements in general tasks, and the opportunities of future research on Code Intelligence.

Terry Yue Zhuo, Ph.D student, Monash University & CSIRO's Data61
Email: terry.zhuo@monash.edu
Website: https://terryyz.github.io/
Terry Yue Zhuo is a Ph.D. student at Monash University and a researcher at CSIRO's Data61. His main research interests are code reasoning, code generation, and LMs for software engineering. Terry is currently supported by Data61 PhD Scholarships, IBM PhD Fellowship Awards, and Google Research Scholar Program. He is an active contributor to the BigCode organization and has been involved in or led various projects like StarCoder, StarCoder2, OctoPack, Astraios, BigCodeBench, and BigCodeArena. He has served multiple times as Area Chair for ACL Rolling Review and now serves as a Senior Area Chair for EMNLP 2025.

Qian Liu, Research Scientist, ByteDance
Email: qian.liu@bytedance.com
Website: https://siviltaram.github.io/
Qian Liu is a research scientist at ByteDance. Before joining ByteDance, he was a joint Ph.D. candidate at Beihang University and Microsoft Research Asia. His

Proceedings of the 2025 Conference on Empirical Methods in Natural Language Processing: Tutorial Abstracts, pages 9–11
November 8, 2025 ©2025 Association for Computational Linguistics

research interests encompass code generation and language models. He has published several papers at top conferences, with notable works including StarCoder, OpenCoder and RegMix. Qian Liu has received several awards such as the KAUST AI Rising Star in 2024, and was nominated for the Baidu Scholarship in 2020. Additionally, he was one of the co-founders of the MLNLP community, a renowned NLP community in China. He has served multiple times as an Area Chair for ACL, EMNLP, and ICLR.

Zijian Wang, Research Scientist Manager, Meta Superintelligence Labs
Email: `zijianwang@meta.com`
Website: `https://zijianwang.me/`
Zijian Wang is a research scientist manager at Meta Superintelligence Labs. Previously, he was an applied scientist manager at AWS AI Labs building models for Amazon Q Developer. His research focuses on building better generative models for code, especially on training, evaluating, and deploying these models at scale. Zijian is an Area Chair of ARR, a lead organizer of Deep Learning for Code (DL4C) workshop at ICLR 2023, ICLR 2025, and NeurIPS 2025, and a co-organizer of LLM4Code at ICSE 2025, a top venue in software engineering.

Wasi Uddin Ahmad, Senior Research Scientist, NVIDIA
Email: `wasiuddina@nvidia.com`
Website: `https://wasiahmad.github.io/`
Wasi Uddin Ahmad is a senior research scientist in the conversational AI research team at NVIDIA. His current research aims to enhance the capabilities of Code LMs in areas such as competitive programming challenges, complex reasoning tasks, and detailed explanation generation, through the use of synthetic data. Prior to his role at NVIDIA, Wasi was at AWS AI Labs, working on code generation for Amazon Q Developer. Wasi obtained a Ph.D. in Computer Science at the University of California Los Angeles. Wasi has published more than 30 research articles in leading NLP, ML, and AI conferences and regularly serves as a program committee member for these venues.

Binyuan Hui, Senior Research Scientist, Meta Superintelligence Labs
Email: `binyuan.hby@alibaba-inc.com`
Website: `https://huybery.github.io/`
Binyuan Hui is a senior research scientist at Alibaba Qwen team, where he leads the development and open-sourcing of the Qwen-Coder series, focusing on enhancing the coding and agent capabilities of large language models (LLMs). Binyuan has made contributions to the open-source code community, including work on projects like StarCoder2, OctoPack, and OpenHands. He has published over 20 papers in

top NLP and AI conferences and has served multiple times as an Area Chair for major venues such as ACL and EMNLP.

Loubna Ben Allal, Research Engineer, Hugging Face
Email: `loubna@huggingface.co`
Website: `https://loubnabnl.github.io/`
Loubna Ben Allal is a research engineer at Hugging Face in the Open Science team, leading efforts on training small language models and creating high-quality pre-training datasets like Cosmopedia and FineWeb-Edu. She was previously a member of the BigCode core team, where she worked on The Stack dataset, the largest open dataset of source code, and co-developed the StarCoder and StarCoder2 models for code generation. Loubna has published several key papers in top AI venues, including NeurIPS and ICLR, and frequently presents her work at global conferences.

Data and Model Centric Approaches for Expansion of Large Language Models to New languages

Anoop Kunchukuttan, Raj Dabre, Rudra Murthy,
Mohammed Safi Ur Rahman Khan and Thanmay Jayakumar

Despite the increasing pace of Large Language Model (LLM) research, a vast majority of existing LLMs mainly support English alongside a handful of high resource languages, leaving a major gap for most low-resource languages. In this tutorial, we focus on approaches to expand the language coverage of LLMs. This provides an efficient and viable path to bring LLM technologies to low-resource languages, instead of training from scratch. We look at approaches at various stages of the LLM training pipeline, like tokenizer training, pre-training, instruction tuning, alignment, evaluation, etc., where adaptations are made to support new languages. We look at data-oriented approaches as well as model-oriented approaches. We hope that our tutorial enables researchers and practitioners to work on incorporating additional languages and tasks into existing LLMs to enhance inclusivity and coverage.

Anoop Kunchukuttan, Principal Applied Researcher, Microsoft
email: `ankunchu@microsoft.com`
website: `https://anoopkunchukuttan.github.io`
Anoop Kunchukuttan is a Principal Applied Researcher in the Core AI group at Microsoft and has worked on Azure Translator for a long time. He is also a co-founder and co-lead at AI4Bharat. His research interests include multilingual learning, machine translation, language modeling and low-resource NLP. He received his Ph.D from IIT Bombay. He has published in ACL, EMNLP, NAACL, TACL, TMLR, AAAI, IJCNLP and CSUR.

Raj Dabre, Research Scientist, Google Deepmind
email: `prajdabre@google.com`
website: `https://prajdabre.github.io`
Raj Dabre is a Research Scientist at Google DeepMind and an Adjunct Faculty at IIT Madras and IIT Bombay, India. He received his Ph.D. from Kyoto University and his Master's from IIT Bombay. His primary interests

Proceedings of the 2025 Conference on Empirical Methods in Natural Language Processing: Tutorial Abstracts, pages 12–13
November 8, 2025 ©2025 Association for Computational Linguistics

are in low-resource NLP, language modeling and efficiency. He has published in ACL, EMNLP, NAACL, TMLR, AAAI, AACL, IJCNLP and CSUR. He is one of the senior leads at the AI4Bharat lab.

Rudra Murthy V, Research Scientist, IBM Research
email: rmurthyv@in.ibm.com
website: https://murthyrudra.github.io
Rudra Murhty is a research scientist at IBM Research since May 2020. He completed his PhD at IIT Bombay under the guidance of Prof. Pushpak Bhattacharyya. He has published in key AI/NLP conferences such as ACL, EMNLP, and NAACL. He has worked in machine translation, named entity recognition, and information retrieval with a focus on Indic languages.

Mohammed Safi Ur Rahman Khan, PhD Student, IIT Madras
email: mohammed.safi@dsai.iitm.ac.in
website: https://safikhansoofiyani.github.io
Mohammed Safi is a PhD student at the Wadhwani School of Data Science and AI, IIT Madras, under the supervision of Prof. Mitesh M. Khapra. He conducts research at the AI4Bharat Lab, with a focus on data-centric approaches and evaluation methodologies for multilingual LLMs. His work on developing large-scale multilingual pre-training and fine-tuning datasets earned the ACL 2024 Outstanding Paper award.

Thanmay Jayakumar, MS Student, IIT Madras
email: thanmayjayakumar@gmail.com
website: https://thanmayj.github.io
Thanmay Jayakumar is an MS student at the Wadhwani School of Data Science and AI, IIT Madras, under the supervision of Prof. Mitesh M. Khapra. His current interests lie in investigating the multilingual capabilities of LLMs and extending their support to low-resource languages, and his work has received the ACL 2024 Senior Area Chair award. He received his B.Tech. from VNIT Nagpur, India, where he worked on image captioning and open-ended information extraction.

Neuro-Symbolic Natural Language Processing

André Freitas, Marco Valentino, Danilo S. Carvalho

Website: `https://sites.google.com/view/nesynlp2025`

Despite the performance leaps delivered by Large Language Models (LLMs), NLP systems based only on deep learning architectures still have limiting capabilities in terms of delivering safe and controlled reasoning, interpretability, and adaptability within complex and specialised domains, restricting their use in areas where reliability and trustworthiness are crucial. Neuro-symbolic NLP methods seek to overcome these limitations by integrating the flexibility of contemporary language models with the control/interpretability of symbolic methods. This hybrid approach brings the promise to both enhance inference capabilities and to deepen the theoretical understanding of LLMs. This tutorial aims to bridge the gap between the practical performance of LLMs and the principled modelling of language and inference of formal methods. We provide an overview of formal foundations in linguistics and reasoning, followed by contemporary architectural mechanisms to interpret, control, and extend NLP models. Balancing theoretical and practical activities, the tutorial is suitable for PhD students, experienced researchers, and industry practitioners.

André Freitas, Research Group Leader at the Idiap Research Institute (Switzerland) and Associate Professor (Senior Lecturer) at the University of Manchester (UK).
email: `andre.freitas@idiap.ch`
website: `https://www.andrefreitas.net`

André Freitas is a and a Research Group Leader at the Idiap Research Institute (Switzerland) an Associate Professor (Senior Lecturer) at the Department of Computer Science at the University of Manchester and an AI Group leader at the National Biomarker Centre (CRUK Manchester Institute). He leads the Neuro-symbolic AI Lab. His main research interests are on enabling the development of AI methods to support abstract, flexible and controlled reasoning. In particular, he investigates how the combination of neural and symbolic paradigms can deliver better models of reasoning. He is an active contributor to the main conferences and journals in the AI/Natural Language Processing (NLP) interface (ACL, EMNLP, EACL, COLING, TACL, Computational Linguistics, AAAI, NeurIPs), with over

Proceedings of the 2025 Conference on Empirical Methods in Natural Language Processing: Tutorial Abstracts, pages 14–15
November 8, 2025 ©2025 Association for Computational Linguistics

100 peer-reviewed publications.

Marco Valentino, Assitant Professor (Lecturer) at the University of Sheffield (UK).
email: `m.valentino@sheffield.ac.uk`
website: `https://www.marcovalentino.net/`
Marco is a lecturer in the School of Computer Science at the University of Sheffield. His research focuses on developing the next generation of AI systems that can use explanatory inference as a core mechanism for learning and reasoning in natural language, particularly in complex domains such as science, mathematics, and healthcare. To this end, he investigates the integration of neural and symbolic AI methods to enhance the robustness and faithfulness of AI-generated explanations and, ultimately, to uncover the principles governing the explanatory inference process in humans. He regularly contributes to major AI and NLP conferences, including AAAI, ACL, EMNLP, NAACL and EACL. Marco was involved in the organisation of workshops, including MathNLP (EMNLP 2022 and 2025, LREC-COLING 2024), and TextGraphs (COLING 2022 and ACL 2024), and tutorials, including *"Reasoning with Natural Language Explanations"* at EMNLP 2024.

Danilo S. Carvalho, Principal Clinical Informatician, National Biomarker Centre, University of Manchester (UK).
email: `danilo.carvalho@manchester.ac.uk`
website: `https://danilosc.com`
Danilo is a Principal Clinical Informatician (Researcher) at the National Biomarker Centre, Cancer Research UK - Manchester Institute, at the University of Manchester, working on *Safe and Explainable Artificial Intelligence (AI) architectures*, centred on generative AI for biomarker discovery and analysis. His main research subject is *Representation Learning*, from the meaning of words to gene interactions, for supporting controlled inference and discovery on large scale data, with emphasis on conceptual interpretation with controlled inference over complex concept spaces. He has experience in both industry and academia, having presented works at multiple AI/NLP international conferences over the past 10 years, such as EACL, COLING and ESANN.

Continual Learning of Large Language Models

Tongtong Wu, Trang Vu, Linhao Luo, and Gholamreza Haffari

Website: https://monashnlp.github.io/monashnlp/cl4llm/

As large language models (LLMs) continue to expand in size and utility, keeping them current with evolving knowledge and shifting user preferences becomes an increasingly urgent yet challenging task. This tutorial offers a comprehensive exploration of continual learning (CL) in the context of LLMs, presenting a structured framework that spans continual pre-training, instruction tuning, and alignment. Grounded in recent survey work and empirical studies, we discuss emerging trends, key methods, and practical insights from both academic research and industry deployments. In addition, we highlight the new frontier of lifelong LLM agents, i.e., systems capable of autonomous, self-reflective, and tool-augmented adaptation. Participants will gain a deep understanding of the computational, algorithmic, and ethical challenges inherent to CL in LLMs, and learn about strategies to mitigate forgetting, manage data and evaluation pipelines, and design systems that can adapt responsibly and reliably over time. This tutorial will benefit researchers and practitioners interested in advancing the long-term effectiveness, adaptability, and safety of foundation models.

Tongtong Wu, Postdoctoral Research Fellow, Monash University
email: tongtong.wu@monash.edu
website: https://wutong8023.site
Dr. Tongtong Wu is a Research Fellow at Monash University. His research focuses on enabling AI systems to perceive, memorize, reason, and adapt within evolving environments, based on his long-term work in continual learning and knowledge graphs. He has coauthored foundational survey work on continual learning in LLMs. He is an editorial board member of Data Intelligence and a reviewer for top-tier journals like TKDE. He also serves on the program committees of the top conferences, including ICML, ICLR, NeurIPS, ACL ARR, AAAI, and IJCAI.

Trang Vu, Lecturer, Monash University
email: trang.vu1@monash.edu
website: https://trangvu.github.io

Proceedings of the 2025 Conference on Empirical Methods in Natural Language Processing: Tutorial Abstracts, pages 16–17
November 8, 2025 ©2025 Association for Computational Linguistics

Dr. Trang Vu is a Lecturer in the Department of Data Science and AI at Monash University. Her work focuses on the intersection of NLP and machine learning, particularly in developing models that generalize across tasks and domains, and building trustworthy and efficient learning systems. She has published extensively in NLP and AI venues and is committed to advancing adaptive and robust AI technologies.

Linhao Luo, Postdoctoral Research Fellow, Monash University
email: `linhao.luo@monash.edu`
website: `https://rmanluo.github.io`
Dr. Linhao Luo is a Research Fellow at Monash University, working on large language models, knowledge graphs, and graph neural networks. His research aims to bridge symbolic and neural representations, with several publications in leading conferences and journals such as ICLR, ICML, ACL, EMNLP, IJCAI, and TKDE.

Gholamreza Haffari, Professor, Monash University
email: `gholamreza.haffari@monash.edu`
website: `https://rezahaffari.github.io`
Prof. Gholamreza (Reza) Haffari is a Professor in the Department of Data Science & AI at Monash University, where he leads the Vision & Language Group. His research focuses on generative AI, multimodal reasoning, and safe continual alignment in LLMs. He is an ARC Future Fellow and has served on senior program committees for top-tier AI conferences. His work is supported by grants from DARPA, Google, eBay, and Amazon.

Author Index